Miss Polite's Stained Heart

Kiddada Asmara Grey

Copyright 2025 Kiddada Asmara Grey
All rights reserved. No part of this publication may be reproduced, distributed or transmitted in any form or by any means, including photocopying, recording, or other electronic or mechanical methods, without the prior written permission of the publisher, except in the case of brief quotations embodied in critical reviews and certain other non commercial uses permitted by copyright law.

Although the author and publisher have made every effort to ensure that the information in this book was correct at press time, the author and publisher do not assume and hereby disclaim any liability to any party for any loss, damage, or disruption caused by errors or omissions, whether such errors or omissions result from negligence, accident, or any other cause. Adherence to all applicable laws and regulations, including international, federal, state and local governing professional licensing, business practices, advertising, and all other aspects of doing business in India, UK, US, Canada or any other jurisdiction is the sole responsibility of the reader and consumer. Neither the author nor the publisher assumes any responsibility or liability whatsoever on behalf of the consumer or reader of this material. Any perceived slight of any individual or organization is purely unintentional. The resources in this book are provided for informational purposes only and should not be used to replace the specialized training and professional judgment of a health care or mental health care professional. Neither the author nor the publisher can be held responsible for the use of the information provided within this book. Please always consult a trained professional before making any decision regarding the treatment of yourself or others.

For more information - kg2educate@gmail.com

There have been times in my life when I felt unsure of myself, my path, my very words. Growing up, I never quite fit in, except within the world I built for myself—a world of books and words, a safe haven I still inhabit today. My other refuge has been the strength of extraordinary women, especially my great-grandmother, my grandmother Violet Claxton, and my extraordinary mother, Yvonne Grey. They taught me the courage to endure, to keep faith, to be vulnerable, to cry and weep and begin again.

Countless people have shaped me over the years. It's impossible to name them all, but I want to express my gratitude to a few. JT, thank you for keeping me grounded in Colorado all those years ago, and for telling me my voice needed to be heard. Your patience and encouragement meant the world to me.

To my sisters, J King, Jennifer Smith, and Jennifer Simmons: you introduced me to new ideas, reminded me I was loved, and always believed in my dreams. I would cross oceans for you.

To the men who have loved me, challenged me, hurt me, held me, and made me weep. Thank you. You've shown me the heights and depths of human connection.

To the women who inspire me daily with your resilience, who create something out of nothing, who survive heartbreak, violence, and the agony of misplaced love: you are warriors. You carry on with grace and strength, caring for your families, friends, and communities. THANK YOU.

To my uncles Junie, Frank, and Mopstik Claxton: thank you for shaping me into the woman I am today, filled with pride, Caribbean spirit, and sweetness. THANK YOU.

To my editor and fellow sistergirl in writing Snehal Singh, THANK YOU for making the magic happen. You don't know the gift you have provided me with this book.

To Maxx, the big sister I always longed for, and God knew I needed: THANK YOU will never be enough.

To all the teen mothers who are told their dreams no longer matter: DON'T believe it. You are precious, and a blessing to the world.

To humanity, our community: it's a miracle we're still standing. Can we remember we are all made from the same dust, just colored with different crayons?

We are called to be better. Thank you for all the chaos, the highs and lows, that fuel my fire to write, to speak out, and to fight against the darkness in the world.

To the one who has held my hand, shared my tears, cheered me on, held me tight, and assured me I can always move forward knowing you have my back: thank you and love you don't even begin to cover it.

Be grateful, diplomatic and gracious.
- Kiddada Asmara Grey

Contents

BROWN GIRL IN THE RAIN	7
LITTLE DADA	9
JUST A PRETTY GIRL	14
GOLDEN	15
LOVE INTERVIEW	16
ODORS OF LOVE	18
GOD DON COME, HE SEND	19
CAME	20
PICTURE	22
BEDTIME CHATTER	23
AUDACITY	24
STAINED HEART	26
GRIEF	27
THUNDER AND LIGHTENING	28
IF I WERE A SOLDIER	30
STAND IN YOUR PAIN	32
SOUND OF RAIN	33
AMERICA II	34
BOHEMIAN RHAPSODY SOCIAL JUSTICE/POLITICAL	37
HEAD NODS ARE NOT UNIVERSAL	38
I SEE YOU SIS!!	40
BLACK CARD	43
AMERICA'S IRONIES"	46
LYNCHED LYNCHED!!!!	47
ODE TO NAT TURNER: A BLACK MAN'S TEARS	48
PLASTICITY	50
THE HANDS THEY HOLD	53

MY DUDE	57
EARTH'S DANCE	58
PEACEFUL JOGS	59
DREAMING	62
UNSAID THINGS	63
YOU KNOW MY ACHE	64
8/30	65
LOVE DESERT	66
MURMURS	69
POEM #1	70
DO MEMORIES EVER DEFLATE	71
NOVEMBER 28	72
LISTEN	73
DIVINE	74
ABOUT THE AUTHOR	75

BROWN GIRL IN THE RAIN

I grew up thinking I was the Morton Salt Girl

Carrying an umbrella sheltering me from the rain I

jumped in puddles in black patent leather shoes

dressed in white socks trimmed in pink lace

and wearing a yellow raincoat

That was me

I just knew it

Every time my mother seasoned food, I saw myself

But I never did play

I wanted to play as a little girl

My goal was to play in the rain

Yet, I was confused

I didn't realize my skin color was not the color of salt

Nor my hair of stringy yellow yarn

Instead, I had black coco puffs

My Mommy brushed with hot water and grease every other day

I yearned to jump in puddles

My adulthood yearns to play

I want to play

Instead, adult fears come forward

Leading me to shake and cry under my weighted blanket

When I close my eyes,

Miss Polite's Stained Heart

I see her

the little black girl

holding her umbrella

wearing patent leather shoes

Muddied and dirty

I am jealous

Continually trying to stay clean

LITTLE DADA

I

I see the little girl with a perfect line splitting her hair into two afro puffs

Staring up the tallest flight of stairs she has ever seen

Her little feet are dressed in patent leather mary janes and soft pink anklet frilled with lace

She is dressed in her soft burgundy overcoat

She is staring up into the heaven of steps and looks a bit confused I know she is wondering how and why?

How long will it take?

Why does she have to go?

Her chocolate face with vaselined lips turns left to right looking for assistance

There is none to be found

She doesn't feel panicked

She just stares up and wonders who is up there

II

I look downward and wonder about the flight of steps Questioning how the hell did I get up here I would never climb this steep hill

My fear of heights is too raw to make that journey I am assured of a tumble and fall

Below I see a dot

And it looks like it moving

There is nothing around me

No light

No darkness

Just steps and a damn dot

This must be a cruel joke

I don't feel alone

I feel safe and unsure unabashedly

I feel stuck and trapped

On the highest level

Of these golden steps

That seems to glimmer and dim at intervals I lift my foot and see the dot move

I wasn't expecting that

Now I am curious

III

The little girl takes a step unwillingly

Yet she feels called to proceed

She realizes the steps light up when she moves forward She is intrigued

This is a game

Maybe this is a puzzle

She likes puzzles

She decides she wants to see the steps gleam with gold And proceeds forward

IV

Now I am scared

Miss Polite's Stained Heart

I don't want to move

Every time I move

It moves

That is not natural

I hesitate and my heart races

Yet,

Yet,

I feel compelled to move

I take a step

Burst into tears

That dot is moving

It seems to be getting closer

When it moves, the steps gleam of gold Just as it does when I move

I feel hopeful

We are moving toward each other

Every step feels like a decade of my life My heart races

I am sweating

I decide to sit on the steps

The black dot keeps moving and is getting closer I can't move anymore

I am stuck in wonderment

V

The little girl is so excited

She hops onto each step

Squealing with delight as she is rewarded With each propulsion

She notices something ahead

She is excited!!!

She delights at the thought of meeting something

She wonders is it an angel

or a ghost

or a monster

Wait a monster?

No

Monster's don't like gold steps and bright things She decides whatever it is

It is safe

She likes everyone

She keeps climbing and

She sees a woman sitting

That is a GROWN woman

The little one wonders why she is crying She seems scared

The little girl is confused

Why would anyone cry on the gleaming steps?

VI

I look up as the tears are streaming down my face I am stuck, afraid and feeling helpless

I see a little girl standing before me

Her patent leather shoes look familiar

Her soft burgundy coat reminds me of kindergarten I am puzzled and confused

She is familiar

There is one step between us

She is smiling at me

Face beaming and highlighted by the gleaming step she is standing on

I realize my step is gleaming too

I stand up with all my courage

Her familiarity is comforting

Her smile echoes safety

I take a step

She steps too

I reach for her hand

She takes it

VII

She disappeared

I finally met me

JUST A PRETTY GIRL

I never thought that I was gorgeous

Just pretty girl, pretty

if you know what I mean

Not too glam or drop-dead gorgeous

Do we even know what we look like?

When our eyes see our reflection in the mirror, we are distorted and fractionated

We don't see who we are

Then we add fake stuff and claim that is who we look like I am confused

I am at fault as well to

I chase the perfect image of myself with my favorite lip glosses, head tilt, and correct lighting

I attempted duck lips once

I realized Daffy and I don't go together

So my lips will continue to rest atop each other as God intended

GOLDEN

In the moments

when silence is golden

Echoes of unruly words

Dance on tympanic airwaves

LOVE INTERVIEW

I want to ask you many questions

Do you love me, or do you like the idea of owning me?

Do you want the bad days, the missed moments, the tears, the stomping feet?

Can I command the gifts of your heart for an answer?

Does your heart have space for the long nights and days of simple moments or the routine of daily life?

Coffee mornings?

Chicken and rice bowls for lunch?

Salmon Dinners?

Does your heart only like shiny new things that make your blood rush through your veins and tear your arteries apart?

Do you prefer breathless moments with quicken paces?

Or do you prefer silent gazes that speak in love languages, making the tip of your heart tremble enough to invite historical memories?

Does your heart know how to stop pleasing all in the big things and little spaces?

I love you

I run away from you

Don't you understand my steps are ordered in the wet concrete of love?

I reverberate in your presence and by your touch

What do you know about tantric lovemaking

Where prayers for the offering of love are given to the most High
Where eyes gaze upon your beloved

Disregarding faults

Where breath meets cells, expanding your lungs

Where unsaid words are written, dancing on fingertips along the slope of arched backs

As praises of your muscular frame toil and bow to the magic you build

I am afraid to open my heart

I keep it on a clock

Open but not 24 hours

Just enough for part-time

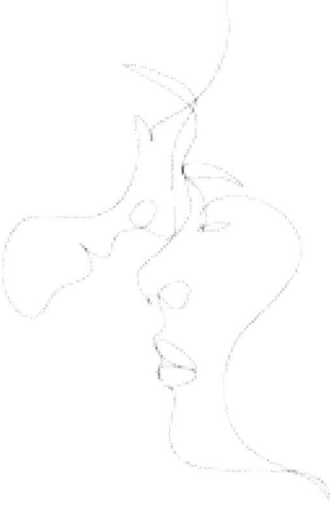

ODORS OF LOVE

I find myself returning to questions from years ago

Why am I here my heart?

My heart doesn't feel like I'm back at the beginning, Full of Shame, sadness, joy, and more

My heart is full of ghosts

filled chambers with golden jewels of memories

brimming with laughter, hand-holding, and quiet moments

Buried hurts dance with bones,

trying to determine who gets to lead this romance

You are both my ghost and chamber

The pieces of my heart are full of fear and hopelessness Yer, the Baseline rhythms of my heart spike

Sometimes

My veins are full of leaves trembling like a shaken tree that prevents me from getting up

Is love supposed to be wrapped between sheets and blankets Or in the trapped odors of memories

GOD DON COME, HE SEND

Brown girl in the rain

Splashing to your beat

Innocent, starry-eyed, full of whimsy

Let your reflection guide you

See your cocoa skin and see your Mommy, auntie and grands

You won't understand for many moons to come

How dancing in chocolate puddles is fantasy

The color of your skin stitches your joy, pain and forever hurts

Forever Hurts are lasting little sister

Embrace them as they make you taller when you feel like a little bit

Enlighten sunbeams to shake the petals on leaves as introductions
Guiding safe passage during the darkest storms

Let your Daddy bless you as clouds meet the night

Before he drops you unto the whitest peaks

Make Mommy your best sistergirl as she swirls in secrets laced in Zora's tongue

You are covered in Sojourner's Truths

Masai jumping like sugar cane soldiers

Maya's love of failures and success

And

Judy saying, "God don come, he send"

For wetness can't harm you

CAME

I knew when he came for me

Cool breeze

Light touch

I felt it

I felt him

Swift, quiet, peaceful

He came for me and I allowed it

In the darkness

Melting forming shadows

Over my 5'2 chocolate frame

Committing black-on-black crimes Claiming and taking me

I was open

He fucked my safe spaces

Using my safe words to open guarded walls

Unwrapped

Raw dogged

Bent over

He broke me

I didn't know I was broken

Until I oozed

I should have been mad

But I wasn't

Miss Polite's Stained Heart

The ocean is liquid

And makes great waves

Water is liquid

And shape shifts

Rain is liquid

And feeds the earth

I became profoundly wet

PICTURE

I could fight with you every day

And my heart will experience joy and pain Concurrently

Remembering when you held me In your arms

Kissing me as we floated

Together under the

Azure skies and Castellano sun

Yet, yearning for an apology

For the waterfall of tears and bad decisions In the name of your safe heart

Not curating mine

Our love is like

Dualing pirate ships

Cresting above the rising gale

Cannons at the ready

With fire-lit balls and explosive love

When do we cruise along like the love boat Sailing on the deep blue sea,

Rocking, rocking as the waves caress Our fears

As they float away

BEDTIME CHATTER

We sat in bed talking and piecing together bits of conversation He told me I was the kind of woman that teaches a man how to love The type of woman who holds a quality that mothers don't provide for their sons

Speechless and quiet in the moment

I wondered how he could say that to me

I was not worthy or deserving of that type of love tribute

I have hurt you

I don't trust you

You don't trust me

Not sure if I love you

Yet, you want to compliment me

AUDACITY

Floating back into time

Riding fluffy white clouds

Slowly melting back into pillows Forgetting rhythmic swish of hips (beating)

Movements that beat in synch Of whirling fans

Sweat and soul glow

Enwrapping your shape

As you steady yourself above me Time is presently awake

Staring at me digitally

Accepting you

Forgetting you

Gathering me

Still wet

Shaken

Dripping as

I gather myself

I open the door

I left me

In the air that you breathe

Sleep with

Brush with

I left me

on the bearer of future children hard and glistening

As you fumble with your phone Telling me that my Lyft was Outside

STAINED HEART

I wish the sun wouldn't shine because it illuminates your missing shadow

Instead, a rainy day could mix with the droplets of tears running down my cheeks

I could wail amidst thunderclaps as a drummer beats upon a bass drum in the background

Loneliness can't hide in the sunshine

GRIEF

Grief is like a fairytale

Encountering each of your steps with expectation To see you standing by the doorway

Your presence embodies the Ghost of Christmas past I can see you there

I can feel you there

I can smell you there

Yet, the candle of your image is only illuminated in my mind

Grief is unfair

The blame of who left and why they left

Is wrapped in the lies of being a bastard turned into a saint Oh, your memory is precious to me!

Grief scrubs the negative, the hurt, and

Angry words

THUNDER AND LIGHTENING

It was time to tell the whole truth and nothing but the truth/ she told herself as she sat trembling and trying to control the rising tide of fear in the lowest pits of her stomach / She heard the rolling tide of thunder and snapping whips of lightning outside of her window/ She could no longer fight the snapshot of a few years ago as she was hidden in the college dorm suite bathroom/ Protect herself from her enraged boyfriend/Not understanding if safety was near

Even though she sat on her bed covered in white sheets and white blankets to provide safety and comfort for herself/ she felt as if she was sitting on the cold, hard floor of her college dorm suite bathroom / The smell of Comet wafting through the air /Recalling the outline of the open under-shelf cabinets of the sink that held her four roommates magical accoutrements/ Making their skin glow/creating magical beings as they trudged to classes every morning

Living with sistergirls is always an adventure/ In this adventure she always walked alone

No one knew she was hiding in the bathroom from the she man loved/As her banged on the door/ The echoing still thumped at the back of her head / in concert with the sound of the thunder and lightning/ rolling through the wind

The bathroom hides in her abuse

She counted the number of times he pounded for her to open the door /Once/twice/ fifteen times/ his voiced enraged/ After the sixteenth pounding, his voice became softer/ and she looked toward the door /She was like Pavlov's dog answering the call to his voice/ Her heart soft/She knew the sobs were coming/Then his apologies/ he was sorry/ he loved her /He lead her heart with each word back to him/convincing her to open the door

The tiny white tiles she sat upon reminded her every time she opened the door and fell for his the tears because each jagged edge of the tile digging into her behind spoke of her daily uncomfortableness of her secret failure of walking away

It was a cold hard truth as her fear shook her

IF I WERE A SOLDIER

If I were a soldier

My PTSD would be acceptable

1 minute

10 minutes

2 years

26 years

A flashback

A glance

A thunderstorm

But I am not

I engaged in war

Hidden deep in the trenches

Cried as the blows came

pummeling from above

But I am not a Soldier

No band of brothers to encourage and salute me Wave flags in memoriam in May for my dutiful service My deaths are not honored

Marching bands don't high step

Down crowded streets lined with proud Americans I hide my wounds

I am quiet and rebuild

I celebrate my navigational skills

Through terrorized spaces

Miss Polite's Stained Heart

In my head

I heal slowly

Courageously

Without my own holiday

I am a victim

Abused

A Survivor

STAND IN YOUR PAIN

Betrayal is the constellation of burning stars

Leaving toxic fumes amidst their twinkling beauty

Sadness lights the skies as Goddess Miseria pours her cup into the night

Love stares with blank eyes

Comforting kisses that feel like icicles

It is hard to sing notes when stumbling feet dance in stiletto heels

The sun can't burn hot enough

when I am cold

SOUND OF RAIN

I awoke to the sound of rain dripping on the trees and creating the initial song of the day

Today's song is a whimper of sad notes and melodies I cried along with the measure of staccato moments

I didn't intend to be mournful today but my soul is panicky my heartbeat cant regulate itself amidst injustice and terror

How can history be corrected when someone will always lose? How does one less bullet raise the dead of injustice killings? How do financial reparations give us our original names?

The world is getting ready to snap

lose its shit

pressure is going to buss the pipes

How much more can we bend?

we know the adjustments of the world

Some of us have practiced backward bends all our lives Some spend their lives upright with indignant righteousness

AMERICA II

We have complex, frightening, and exciting days ahead of us We need to stride in step

Get ready

But first

I need you to stop, sit down in a comfy chair, and relax Get close to the edge of the seat and place your hands on your lap Square your shoulders

Sit up tall

And breathe with me

Inhale through each of your nostrils

Allow your first breath to expand your ribs so much that it hurts You are reminded of the days ahead

Exhale

Remember and contemplate each step you will have to take Now, take your second deep breath

Inhale until your genes swell

You are growing

Getting larger

You are full

Exhale

Your frame carries the DNA of the Clotida Take your third breath

This is your healing breath

Imagine taking the hand of your sister or brother Feel their pulse

Feel their warmth

Let the oxygenated cells regenerate

Creating symbiosis

Our journey is one

We can do this

Together

For Us

For our absence in America

Exhale to be seen

To be cemented in stars

on sidewalks

In the airwaves

In the airwaves

On billboards

mail pieces

Barbershops and beauty salons

For those whose hands picked cotton

For Reconstruction Senators who were forced into the erasure of progress

History is now

Recline in your chair

Cradle your body amongst the wings

Think about the humming, soothing power surging through your body

Let each breath be your guide

Let each breath re-energize your momentum

For her

America

BOHEMIAN RHAPSODY
SOCIAL JUSTICE/POLITICAL

Let me make a call, she said, as she secretly rang the police

A 12-year-old boy waited on the porch anxiously to confirm a donation to basketball camp

Blue sirens wailed as they pulled in front of the manicured lawn, three-story brick townhome on

5280 Forrest Lane

There stood a 5'6 black male standing in front of the glass Perroki door, hulking and bulking at 265 pounds, peering, lurking

They yelled for his attention,

He didn't give it

They yelled again

His iPhone earbuds bumping to trap music

He didn't hear the call to identify

He stood at the door intently,

Awaiting the lovely lady who said she needed to grab her purse

He died on her doorstep

Reaching to fix

His ear pod

Agitating his ear

HEAD NODS ARE NOT UNIVERSAL

I took a sojourn

And entered into Black Paris

Excited to be surrounded by blackness passerby's on the cobbled streets In the boutiques

Underground in the Metro

I was gleeful

happy that I saw other

Black faces

A mirror image of me

Men in gold-laced thobes

Rocking Yankee baseball hats

I heard old school hip hop

East coast lyrics

On French airwaves

I slowly nod my head

And tip my left eye

Of a sly secret known only to

those with melanated skin

Executed with dead-ass perfect eye contact

To my surprise

I received blankness

The mirror was deceptive

Miss Polite's Stained Heart

I was not seen

In fact I was

Sent through

Like when children snap at each other

"Your Momma is made of glass"

Well I met my Momma

A clean-cut sear

So hot it didn't even hurt

I was confused

I needed to try this again

Targeted specifically to sistergirls

Large afros, braided hair, pressed chic bobs of all shades French-speaking sometimes with hints of Arabic Clear skin, lips popping

I stealthily nodded again

A little head tilt

With a bit of

I SEE YOU SIS!!

Still… Nothing

Is it just me?

My need for recognition

Was my black American handbag

Slung on my shoulder

Well, now it slipped off

Black folks supposedly,

allegedly

love a good head nod

It recognizes injustices

Blessings that we are still standing The low-key hey boo, i see you

An honorific of blackness

A prideful roar

Of the ancestors and descendants That we are still motherfucking standing A fuck this government and oppression

An unending loss of what I can or can't do Injustices with dripping moments of triumph I am lost and sad

I pivoted to soothe my ego attended A French black experience tour

I knew I would find blackness there!

I was reminded the French

believed they were all one

Liberté, Égalité, Fraternité

The right to live freely

Equality for all

Solidarity for a free and fair society Maybe black folks in France believed this Or maybe they achieved it

Except I saw black immigrants protesting Immigrants are politically weaponized

by every politician in France

And marches are itchy reminders of the dire straits and unfair treatment of new blacks

Into the French society

The belief of equality seems to be the only answer Why my head nod was not returned

Liberty? Equality? Fraternity?

Where blackness is no longer an otherness

Where blackness melts into colorless

Where mirrored reflections are no longer needed Oneness

Maybe the black French I encountered

Didn't see the blackness on me

Only in me

I was the same as anyone else

Like the pure definition of white folks

Saying, "I don't see color"

However, I suffer under the thought

Of being colorless

Or bewildered about the idea of living in a nation Being fully accepted and understood

Miss Polite's Stained Heart

I am jealous and skeptical

I understand the low-key falsehood

and trap of wanting hope

Then I saw the black Sudanese men protesting My brothers!

I saw y'all

I recorded that shit

Cause that was not equalite!

Maybe they have not been provided

The manual of acceptance of the French motto Or maybe they are not the correct type of black yet? My optimism is on fleek

Oh! the possibilities

I want equality in the United States

I want freedom and justice for all

I also need my head nod

BLACK CARD

I am turning in my black card

I don't want the rewards points, prizes nor credibility That comes with being a cardholder

I am done

I can't keep up

Blackness has gotten out of control

I can't keep up

The super woke

Sisters and brothers changed the game

My blackness was dem and we

Bob Marly and a good jump up

Curry goat, oxtail and Ting

Intertwined with Self-Destruction, Big Daddy Kane and Erik B Pan-Africanism, seeking history about Jomo Kenyatta, Haille Selaisse,

(Jah Rastafari)

And understanding the roots that grew big trees where leaves and branches held

The privilege of time

I got that Blackness

Purchasing one-dollar Final Call papers sold by

The sharpest bowtie-wearing negros

Musing at the 5 percenters and the 12 tribes of Israel brothers on the street corners and subway stops wearing

Brocade tassels battling who is the foundational realest of mankind
Speaking to communities who are seeking something– A pathway

A foundation

An identity

Out of depicted mediocrity and self-unknowing I understood when Ronnie, Bobbie, Ricky and Mike showed Concern about not reaching the girl of their dream Yep

I understood all 'a dat

You didn't think I had it in me did you?

Yes, I have the dem, we and dat in me

(Before I go any further)

This is the part of the presentation

Where ankles get broken

Negros cry and get in their feelings

I might get canceled

I

Don't

Care

It is what it is

See, I knew things were changing

When I was spelled "eye"

People no longer understand but

Overstand?

Where my womanhood was not just introduced By womb and became wombman

Miss Polite's Stained Heart

I am confused

Or when the sun, the moon and the stars aligned at Night for celestial beings to guide brothers and sisters Back to the homeland

To when we all became kings and queens

Consuming more than just tea

This don't make no damn sense

Some of use on the coast had to go fish

Or out in the bush hunting for wild boar and scrounging for vegetables and praying for rain

How sway?

I prefer to reign with logic not made up

Grand Risings to pacify

My people say

You have to go to the root

The root bears fruit

From planting seeds to bearing fruit

How did we accept shame

For building a nation

To black women are the destruction of black men Fake doctors healing people and becoming politicized Not understanding weaves are natural to Africans Just as blue eyes can thrive against our hue

Leading to natural curly hair is a foe

and falling

In love with a stripper is a matter of

Personal agency

AMERICA'S IRONIES"

Satan walks into a synagogue and kills Jewish elders who survived concentration camps

The President of the United States holds his scepter in tribute Wildfires spread in the suburbs, killing mass amounts of people, and causing significant losses of homes

and

The President of the United States ignites the flame of atrocities with his very own gold-plated lighter

A young black activist, in the prime of his life, fights for black justice and recurrences of the historical past,

is found hanging from a tree;

LYNCHED LYNCHED!!!!

Why would an activist lynch himself to honor the slave masters?

Bemused Lyndon B Johnson was surprised to discover poor whites also had their votes suppressed as false equality reigned in the face of the 1965 Voting Rights legislation

Conservative Christians have replaced the Psalms with White Nationalism and hate gospel

Jesus Christ, our Lord, and Saviour, climbs off the cross to watch redemption and forgiveness burn like a Saturday night at a Klan rally God Bless America

ODE TO NAT TURNER: A BLACK MAN'S TEARS

Scared little boy hiding from manhood

Vulnerability never introduced

Trying to define what it means to be a man

A free man

The cotton fields, the cane fields, the night into day, the days burning into nights

the incessant yes's that never seem right

no thank you's

just servitude

Tears fall when your woman, your tastes, your sounds, your pleasures

are taken and given to another Man and Master

Children you love half belong to you

Friendships at birth that turn into hate into teenage hood

The shining sun on your back glows as the blood drips from your fingertips

Weeping

Weeping

Weeping

As the cotton bushel needs to be 10 more pounds today The sweat falling deep within the crevice of your back Has more freedom than you

Marking its place on the earth

Cry! Because you swing in trees

And can't swing on trees

Cry! because you birthed the Nation

And the tossed afterbirth is you

Cry! and weep, my brother

The globe that falls down your cheek

carries the world

PLASTICITY

Sisters have you ever sat down, listened to, and engaged in conversation with black men

I don't mean like we are drinking and talking shit type conversation

I am talking about the type of conversations when they open the deep abyss of darkness

and allow the light to shine through for a few moments where you know their hearts beat and in need of repairs

The place where the 12-year-old boy still wonders about his body holds his Mommy's hand

and cries when the world seems too big

and is crushing his soul

When their manhood is gleaming bright in the safety of womanhood
Not downtrodden by toxic masculinity playing tunes in his head arresting his words

living in flats and not high notes

Sister girls, this is when we need to listen and be blessed

Brothers will shoot their shots on how Mommy and daddies' love created them and shape-shifted their lives

The sacredness of parentage love is all-knowing and powerful Their faces transform from what is to be a man

to the courageous man

who lets his emotions guide him without fear

Revelations of shame and disappointment creep out into the light

with hoarse voices that fight back glaciers of tears

melting upon grinding sand

when they did not know what to do

Other than being a "MAN"

Acknowledgments of not having tools other than man privilege which is the elitist and most powerful thing a man has… even a black man

They will lift the veil from your eyes about being afraid to love and not being loved enough

If you are like me, you want to interject and say

"We sisters love you, but you always fight us!"

However, my dear sisters,

One can't love when one cannot define love

Definition is concrete, and love does not have hardness

One cannot accept love when hardness is seamless there are no cracks for love to permeate

Love sits on the surface and coats like oil

It holds in the moisture but damn sure doesn't moisturize

They do reveal how they love us

Coconut oil and shea butter magical natural sisters to the sweet sugar cookie Bath and Body work sisters that leave traces on their pillows despite what the manosphere says

Take a deep breath

Inhale their words

Not mine, but theirs

It is love

Pure black man on black woman love

Love on the brothers

Love on our brothers

Miss Polite's Stained Heart

Black men are magical

I love the spell they put me under

THE HANDS THEY HOLD

As I do my job daily, I pray that I hear all children's and families' voices so that I can make the best decisions

As I begin my day, I know I have chosen this work to grow my understanding of safe, healthy choices and to be a teacher to others in assistance

When I separate little and big hands, I remember I have good intentions

I understand the disconnection of burden, love and hopeful dreams, comfortable surroundings, and false fantasies

I remember I don't intend to do harm

I remember and forgive myself for making imperfect decisions

My eyes believe what I see to be true, and I honor that I may not see everything

I remember the "demons" I protect children were once children who were harmed and loved in unhealthy ways

I remember toxic behaviors have roots and practices in maltreatment, injustice, injury and despair

Yet toxicity has found a home in the softest places of hurting people who grow the poisonous fumes of love

"Don't inhale the love you want", you tell the broken

However, understanding love is in the expansion of DNA from conception to birth and death

I remember, I am not a liberator

I remember, I am not a hero

I remember, I am not a Harmer

Miss Polite's Stained Heart

I am a fixer

I am a hand holder

I am the beginning of justice

Dear Brothers and Sisters

We have complex and exciting days ahead of us

We need to stride in step

But first

I need you to stop, sit down in a comfy chair, and relax Get close to the edge of the seat and place your hands on your lap Square your shoulders

Sit up tall

And breathe with me

Inhale through each of your nostrils

Allow your first breath to expand your ribs so much that it hurts That is to remind you of the days ahead

Exhale and remember the moments each step you will have to take Now take a second deep breath

Inhale until your genes swell,

You feel them increasing your stature

You are growing

Getting bigger

You are full

Exhale

You carry the DNA of the Clotida and our brethren on the front lawn of the

White House when Lincoln proclaimed freedom

Miss Polite's Stained Heart

Take a third breath

This is your healing breath

Imagine taking the hand of your sister or brother

Feel their pulse

Feel their warmth

Let the oxygen regenerate

And create symbiosis

The journey is one

We can do this

Together

For us

For our absence in America

Exhale to be seen

To be stamped on sidewalks

In the airwaves

On billboards

On mail pieces

In barbershops and beauty salons

For the sisters and brothers whose hands picked the cotton for the suits and tees we wear

For the Reconstruction Senators forced out to begin the erasure of progress

History

Is

Now

As you lean back in your chair

Cradle your body amongst your favorite pillows

Think about the humming, soothing power surging through your body

Every minute counts

Let each breath be a guide

Let each touch re-energize your momentum

For her

America

MY DUDE

A man reached down and pulled me Into manhood

I am an elder with a young man's mind As I missed the lessons of wisdom that only come from loving words

Energy charges through my fingertips as his fingers laced around mine Pulling and yanking me toward

the shadowed frame of myself

My vulnerability was encouraged Allowing my soul to weep

With shame, hurt and abandonment I learned to redefine softness as courage

Slickness in the streets

Hustling and bearing seeds

Scars exacerbated my emptiness

It took a handshake

It took a dap

Loving me into manhood

EARTH'S DANCE

The earth spun

And I danced upon its' axis As your words spoke to me Like golden twine

That became my tight rope

PEACEFUL JOGS

I went for my daily jog

running for health

running for a pattern

running with my beats

The pattern of my steps

along the blackened pavement left foot, right foot

right foot, left foot

clipping right along

The trees are my muses

The birds are my symphony Each house is a choir member

I heard a tune

An alto singing a hymn

I followed the hymnal of praise as each note called to me

I yearned for more

I want to envelope her openness

She welcomed me with

wide open arms

warm and bright

Her personality was breezy

she sang without abandonment though I could see she was building herself anew

Her bone structure was concrete but she was missing teeth She was soft

Miss Polite's Stained Heart

but hard to touch

my ears

only heard her sing-song voice

I wanted to stay

and listen to the

operatic tunes

time was not on my side

back to the cacophony

of birds and trees

in their jet-black robes

Their song became my glory

Until I heard a rumble

Something like a cymbal crash

I could no longer hear

My Tympanic Concert

on the pavement

I was asked to dance

My rejection was polite

I was grabbed

A violent dance ensued

Pulling

Tugging

My chest was heavy

Miss Polite's Stained Heart

I spun

and tumbled

A bell rang

and another

I look toward the conductor as he lowered his baton

The curtain closed

DREAMING

Standing still

Watching yourself fall apart Unsure which piece

To catch first

UNSAID THINGS

Partie Once

Yeah, sure

We were cool on the surface

But not in the details

Partie Deaux

Minding your Business

Don't worry about my tears; they are mine to have

Partie Trois

Chocolate

There is something sexy about a black man sitting on a couch with this cologne wafting through the air like being enveloped in melting chocolate

YOU KNOW MY ACHE

No, no, no,

leaves my tongue like a slippery monotone

mired in negative rhymes and notes

flowing through me

8/30

I silently beg

Plead with you to tell me who you are

All of you

Are you afraid this is a test you will fail

I am way beyond quizzes

I tiptoe inside the facts

even though you are a course in relativity

I am not mastering

I awake to puffy swollen eyes

I search my dream to see if you and I had a fight

If we were screaming and crying

If you said something hurtful

If I was disrespectful

If the door slammed

The couch is messy with the pillow and blankets snatched off the bed

Meta morphing into a space of hostility and not comfort

LOVE DESERT

I am afraid to write

I don't know why

but it is not speaking to me

My mental pen is calling and I turn off the ringtone

The truth hurts

Writing is truth

Truth is writing

My truth is not complicated or punishing

However it pulls on the little strings of my heart,

tearing little pieces of strength I thought were in stone I feel pain that is lost in forgiveness and documented in truth

Tears of pain do not fall

Pieces of forgiveness do

My power is in love

A first love

A love that accepts all, denies all and wants all

Deep inside my soul

I cannot describe the emotion

It needs a name, so I will call it,

IT,

I am not angry, fearful or sad

IT presents at the surface

Waiting to spill over but IT does not

So I sit at the window watching dark waves crashing, creating white foam pools

cresting

Under the moon

I am transported to a time and place not lost

but hidden and not in the present

IT only appears with a confession

I confess

I thought

IT was love

Love I deserved not to receive

Another person wanted IT,

Dreamed of IT

Shared IT with me and

Instead, IT was taken from me

A kiss in the darkness

A shudder

a breath leaving hesitantly

and my head spinning

IT was the beginning and the end of all things

The best and worst simultaneously

I am full of wonderment and confidence

that fell from

Miss Polite's Stained Heart

the sky into my lap

I wonder aloud in my head

Love Doesn't

MURMURS

His words never laid enough bricks high enough to prevent my heart from loving you

Words acted like magic spells to build a web of attachment Replacing and not killing the love hidden deep within Jeopardy provides the answers

Questions address missteps when the brain and heart don't fit The brain doesn't retire longing.

Instead, it creates new synapses and maps of a new life Heart murmurs keep you living

With tiny holes that never close

Occasional aches remind you of painful consequences. No need for breathing treatments

When you're not breathing

POEM #1

I knew I missed you

When I couldn't hear

My name dancing on your tongue

DO MEMORIES EVER DEFLATE

Like air slowly released from a balloon Does joy, happiness, frustration or anger Dissipate

I am told memories fade

But where do they go

When memories fails

Do the other participants hold it

Or does it slither back into the ethos For others to gain a new experience Does the cut that wounded deep

Heal itself with the sutures of time Does life return as raindrops in reverse To create fluffier clouds

Does anger wane like boiling water To still water

Can delight ever placate

Emotional lows like tornadic

Hails of exuberance

Memories melt like hot coffee touching skin Leaving a mark and inedible

NOVEMBER 28

Leaning against the beige wall

body crumbled

shoulders curved

Stomach muscles clenched and cramping As she tried to catch her breath

She wept

She wailed

She wailed for him

Crying for him

And he knew it

He wasn't concerned

Arrogant as he steadied her

He was willing to love her through it

LISTEN

That is NOT a love song! Hoteps battling on air about Innerstand as the gateway to the third eye

Hoteps,

Have you forgotten matriarchal societies

Bearing strong women and families

As you denigrated sexual beings

Who shouldn't have menstrual cycles

Yet for all my sexual prowess

And honor as a black queen

You want to prove me with pyramid-forming

Orgasms

On the first date because my job is to procreate?

You can't body shame me and then tell me

What lies between my thighs is heaven and earth Why oh why are the brothers that don't talk

Like you, walk like you called simps?

What is that? I can't inner nor overstand?

The black stripe on my card is worn to the plastic There aren't enough digits in the code to identify this theology Urban dictionary wasn't made for me

DIVINE

Divine spirit created woman

With the pleasures of pink sands

To be a helpmate, creator and builder

Instead her life is full of woe

Her Cries for help silenced by judgment

Bearing the heavy workload of emotional labor and trauma

Silent cries in the shower and in the closet

Hiding from the heaviness of responsibility

Arms wide and strong enough to embrace, cuddle and soothe Not caring that her solitude is being used and abused God created woman in strength

Providing her an extra rib for uncertainty

And carrying dissatisfaction

ABOUT THE AUTHOR

Kiddada Asmara Grey, a descendant of strong Caribbean women, is a writer who channels their resilience and wisdom into her work. Her writing explores the complexities of being a Black woman, navigating the delicate balance of heartache, vulnerability, and unwavering strength.

Grey's debut poetry book, Miss Polite's Stained Heart, delves into the complexities of the human experience, particularly the challenges women face. Her work explores themes of love, loss, social justice, and racial inequality, offering readers a powerful blend of empathy and insight. Committed to social change, Grey uses her platform to give voice to the voiceless, challenge societal norms, and inspire a more equitable world.

Social Media Link

www.ingramcontent.com/pod-product-compliance
Lightning Source LLC
Chambersburg PA
CBHW072024060426
42449CB00034B/2105